DROWNING IN MY OWN SPIT

DROWNING IN MY OWN SPIT

A Collection Of Poems By:
Amber Hasan

3 Pens Publishing
Duluth, GA 30095

www.3penspublishing.com

Published by 3 Pens Publishing
P.O. Box 957687
Duluth, GA 30095

All rights reserved. No part of this publication may be reproduced, stored in a retrieval system, or transmitted, in any form or by any means, electronic, mechanical, photocopying, recording or otherwise without prior permission of the publisher.

In Loving Memory of:
Vanessa Parson, Carrie O. Bates, and Mrs. Annie

Table of Contents

Preface
By Natasha "Theory" Thomas (Neogriot Collective)   i-iv

Diary I - Sometimes I feel like I'm speaking NuShu

1st Poem In Three Years	1-2
Drowning In My Own Spit	3
I Lose Track Of Time Sometimes	4
Learning To Swim	5
Amber at 18 Part 1	6
Amber at 18 Part 2	7
Circa 1995	8
Once Morning (revisited)	9
Confessions Of Isis	10-11
Buckingham Palace	12-13
1605	14
R.I.P.	15
1st Pregnancy	16
Am I Talking To Myself	17
Just A Question	18
Eucharist	19-20
Counting Sacrificial Sheep	21-22
All My Skeletons Won't Fit In My Closet	23-24
Seven Years Bad Luck	25-26
When The Rainbow Is Not Enuf	27-28
Killing Goliath	29
Thank You Marshall Mathers	30
Untitled 1	31-32
Girl Fight	33

Diary II – The Revolution Will Not Be Available On Bootleg

Big Black Truth	37-38
For Bill, Uncle Ric, and Roy II	39-40
I Prefer Kool-Aide	41-42
I Couldn't Carry A Tune In A Suitcase	43-44
Words Of My Father	45
On The Back Of Milk Cartons	46-47

Diary III – Cupid Must Be Cross-Eyed

Something Like A Love Poem	51
Thank You For Laughing At My Jokes	52
We'll Be Butterflies	53
Word Can't Explain	54
Beyond Fear	55
Sun Salutation	56-57
Fallen	58

Diary IV – Life

Amongst The Living	61

Preface

Before I met Amber, I met **Wisdom**.

I was just about to leave the café's monthly poetry night, thinking I couldn't bear to experience anymore of the mahogany monotony and lackluster revolutionary rants. After a 10-hour shift and a headache that was threatening to become a migraine, I decided that I had enough "poetry" for one night. The finger snapping indicating that a poet was exiting the stage was my cue. I tried to make a beeline for the door, intent on getting out before the next name on the list materialized in front of the mic.

I almost succeeded.

Then I heard the exuberant host say, "Come on y'all….give it up for Wisdom!" Something made me stop. To this day, I can't exactly articulate what that *something* was. Perhaps I was intrigued by the metaphoric possibilities of the phrase "give it up for Wisdom." Maybe I slipped into writers' mode and was wondering how I could incorporate such a statement into some future pieces. Or perhaps I wanted to see the person who was supposed to be the living, breathing manifestation of something as intangible as Wisdom. Over analytical to a fault, I wanted to see if the walk matched the talk. I decided that I could not suffer through one more, bad, Love Jones remake, to satisfy my curiosity.

That's when I saw her. Upon hearing her name called, she rose with, what some would call, a contradictory look on her face. She was humble, yet confident, beautiful yet accessible. An odd mix of superwoman strength and black girl vulnerability, she seemed unaware of the fact that all eyes were on her. I wondered how many of the people in the room could see what I recognized instantly. There was nothing contradictory about her blatant duality. Those seemingly conflicting qualities that seemed to define her presence were not conflicting at all. Rather they were the definitive attributes of womanhood, the embodiment of experience, understanding, struggle and will. At that moment, I knew what it felt like to be introduced to Wisdom.
She stepped on stage and proceeded to shatter long-standing preconceived notions with a lyrical sledgehammer. She was quick to let you know that your traditions and expectations did not define the perimeters of her existence. While she appreciated the finger snapping and support, she hated coffee shops and the pretentiousness that seems to accompany them.

Her poetry was not borne of the plush literary womb of academia or lofty abstract idealism. Her words were raised in concrete reality of struggling mother, redeemed thugs, and socio-political critique that made you understand the urgency. Wisdom's words reminded you that while some people use hard knocks as a crutch or a lukewarm excuse for complacency, others use it to become warriors, poets, students, teachers and seekers. Her poetry reminded us of the mythical Phoenix who welcomed every death as a chance for re-birth. As she spit, it was obvious that I was witnessing more than just fancy word play manufactured for audience delight. I was witnessing a self-healing, a cleaning of spiritual wounds with words. I didn't even notice my headache anymore.

By the time she stepped off stage, the audience was dumbstruck. A half second of stunned silence paralyzed the room before we enthusiastically burst into applause. It seems like everybody forgot about the "be-cool" finger snaps. We had been hijacked; unrepentantly ripped away from the façade and forced back into our own skin by the words of this woman. She smiled and thanked us with a humility that was becoming increasingly rare in the ever-growing spoken word circle. I decided that I needed to know Wisdom.

That's when I met Amber. Even though I was amazed by the poet, I am even more amazed at the woman. In the short time that I have known amber, I've seen her march for women's rights in DC, protest the global econo-chauvinism of the IMF and the WTO, create self-empowerment workshops for teen girls, shuttle her students to cultural events that serve to broaden their understanding, organize poetry slams to increase awareness and funding for HIV/AIDS research, and most recently, I've seen her breathe life into Nozake Shange's Lady in Blue in the "New" McCree Theatre's production of "For Colored Girls Who Have Considered Suicide When The Rainbow is Enuff." Unlike many open mic freedom fighters, Amber's call to action doesn't lose steam when she steps off the stage. She lets her life stand as a testament.

Amber does more than write poetry, she creates prosaic masterpieces. Shutting down slam after slam, her name has become synonymous with a force to be reckoned with in the poetry circle. These days, local artists are clamoring to do collaborations with her, wanting to marry the substance of her air to theirs, desiring to have some Wisdom of their own. Fortunately, it seems as if the literary Gods have answered our prayers and have given us Wisdom in a book.

When Amber first gave me the manuscript, I was surprised at what I sw. All poets and spoken word artist know the difference between a poem that works on paper and a spoken word slam piece that works on stage. Reading over the poems in preparation for writing this preface, I was delighted to see that any number of the poems were both literary enough to satisfy the bourgeoisie breed of self-proclaimed poetry pundits who denounced hip-hop flavored spoken word movement, and as well breathed with authenticity and vibrancy that had the "Flintstone" experience written all over them. The material in this book is a beautiful merger of substance and swagger.

"Drowning in My Own Spit" is a chaotic mix of self-exploratory stew. It's honestly and transparency challenges the reader to engage in a parallel probe of their own psyches as Amber delves into her own. In questioning her purpose and mission, she forces us out of the self-protective layers that we have become so accustomed to. It is not a book for the self-delusional. It was not written to make us comfortable. Nor was it written to portray its author as a saint.

Amber's critical analysis of the world doesn't stop a few steps short of her own doorstep. She plows through her own motives and intentions, unmercifully. She's not afraid to be unabashedly human.

In both "I lose track of time" and "Circa 1995", she urges us to see the futility in serving sentences shackled to insecurities, confusion and fear. Time is short, she seems to say, and we can spend it languishing or living, in lunacy or in love, but at the end of the day, the choice and always has been ours. In "Confessions of Isis", she invites:

> *Baby boys circumcised by circumstance*
> *Step into my circumference*
> *And I will lend you my comfort*

Later in that poem, she hints to her deliverance stating:

> *My intention was to remain invisible*
> *But my words go claustrophobic bursting*
> *Out of my mouth before I chocked on reality*
> *Cuz it would really be a shame*
> *For someone to give me the Heimlich*
> *Maneuver and find it was only the truth*
> *Caught in my throat*

Reading through the poems, one gets the impression that Amber is selling us more than poetic observation and reflection, she is selling us redemption and renewal.

As I shifted through the poems that make up this book, I was transported back to the 80's, when another Flint based artist name Breed gained accolades and commercial success with his song entitled "Ain't No Future in Your Frontin", a little ditty lambasting disingenuous fakers. In contrast, Amber honors the truth without hurling judgment arrows and if she did decide to ever pick up a bow, you can almost bet that the first arrow would be self-directed. Like Breed's song, Amber's work encourages us to throw away the facades. However, "Drowning in My Own Spit" is not an accusation. Rather it encourages us all to immerse ourselves in own spirit and to embrace what we find there instead of masking it. It speaks to those who are trying to remember things that they were born knowing and lost somewhere in the process poetry's proliferation of grandiose ghetto gurus It is for those of us wishing to abandon the grandstanding.

It is for those of us who are truly seeking…..WISDOM.

NaTasha "Theory" Thomas
The Neo Griot Performance Collective

Poetry

Is when I let my soul

Bleed into words

And drown the world

With my spirit

Diary I

Sometimes I feel like I'm speaking Nu Shu

First Poem in 3 Years

My journey began where
The truth lies with a severed tongue
And flickering streetlights are my North Star
Staring blindly
Down the road to righteousness
Breath reeking
With the intoxicating stench of ignorance
Like a dead man walking
I was merely an imitation of life
Trying to simulate happiness to simple
For me to understand

It's as if the night was watching me
Watch my life pass me by
And the day kept tabs on my absences
From the living
I was just flesh
My heart pumped blood
And my lungs expanded with air
But I could not feel
All those years of trying to hide
Made my true self disappear

I had lost me
So deep inside of me
That there was no me
Only falsetto visions
Given
Depending on who the viewer was

I sat silent for so long
Swallowing my words
Becoming constipated by my thoughts
Afraid to speak
For fear that someone would listen
For fear that I could no longer hide

So I sat
And I wept
And I died
Traveling aimlessly
Into the hell of my own knowledge
While thirsting to drink
From the well of belief
Then all at once
Fate snatched me from the womb of darkness
Naked and afraid
Then the truth smacked me on the ass
And my body filled with breath
Finally I was alive

Drowning in my own spit

There is so much clutter here
So many words
Phrases
Ideas
So many poems
I could give into this madness
Letting these thoughts incapacitate me
I could let these words bind
Me to pen and paper
Transforming me into eternal poetry
A never-ending rhythm
Deciphering existence
Coming as close to death as earthly as possible
By living words
So many words
So
So many words
Pouring freely
Oceans flowing from my mouth
Me
Drowning in my own spit

I Lose Track of Time Sometimes

Each day I take trips
And reach destinations
And it still takes the best in me
Not to question thee

So I question them
Who twiddle thumbs
While obviously overlooking their own
My hands are all I own
And even those are on loan…

Momma said I would understand
When I was grown
And since I don't plan to stop growing
Then knowing will forever be
Slightly beyond my grasp
My first is my last
And in regards to steps and breaths
My last will most certainly be my best
As long as time is still a test

I plan to study seconds
And cram minutes into my memory
So as not cheat myself
Of the honor of holding hours
Against my bosom
Nursing them until they become days
Weaning them into weeks
Marveling as months grow into years
Yearning for time to take its time
But it won't wait for me

So I create my own space
And get lost somewhere between
Time and space
Riding sound waves
As if they were a deuce and a quarter
Bending celestial corners
Until I reach that parallel universe
Where I finally find myself
Free styling to the melody of life's mysteries
Repeating myself verbatim
Without ever saying the same thing twice

Learning to Swim

As the sun rose
I saw the smile of my child
And it all made sense

Nothing even matters

There is not pain
No struggle
No bad days

They are all figments of my imagination
I must invent the negative
Because life seems to good to be true
And love feels so satisfying
That is seems sinful
Everything is everything
And
Everything is just wonderful

As the the sun set
I saw peace in my sleeping child
And it all made sense

Everything matters

Because even those things that I imagine
Seem magnified on manic Mondays
And black Fridays and even though I am conscious
That I create my own catastrophes
There are still some bridges that I must burn
Because it's the only way I'll learn to swim
So to avoid drowning I become fluently fluid
Now I flow
Like oceans I'm wide open and since the world involves me daily
I'm evolving daily
Exploring myself
From tramp to lady
From babies momma
To daddies baby
And just maybe…
One day this will all make perfect sense

Amber @ 18 Part 1

Removed from my past consciousness
I now realize that I was never conscious at all
Traveling helplessly
In the space between my ears
Shut off from reality
Alone with my thoughts
Baffled by the fact that I really needed love,
I really needed faith,
I really needed someone other than myself
I am not an island

Amber @ 18 Part 2

When the lights came on,
That's when I realized it was dark
And my whole outlook changed like the
Cycles of the moon
My eyes had been wide open
It was my heart that had been shut
Unwilling to be open
Because of the pain that I have felt
Afraid to be alive
Because to be alive is to be human
And to be human is to feel
And to feel is to love
And to love is to hurt eternally
But without the pain from love
Life had no joy

Circa 1995

Blindly in a hurry
Going nowhere fast
Eagerly searching
For what is searching for me
Wildly circling destiny
Never even knowing it was there
Diving in the depths of my own ignorance
Gasping for faith
While trying to stay afloat
On a rickety raft of hope
Believing that all of my pain
Would eat me alive

One Morning (Revisited)

One morning
I heard the truth spoke
It swept through my being
With the power of grandma's hands
As I wept endless tears
About endless troubles

It moved me like the Holy Spirit
On Sundays is small southern towns
Causing me to
Speak tongues of understanding
And praise it without inhibition

It let me experience
As if today is my first day
And these words are my first words,
And this joy is everlasting
Far beyond anything imaginable
It became me
Purposely penetrating the portions
Of me that I'd swept under rugs
Merging I and it, creating us,
So that one morning I could speak the truth

Confessions of Isis

I speak with certain rhythms
It's like your heart toffee in my whisper
My words sprinkle a candy reign
Men they call it chocolate thunder
Like my eyes
Hold the eighth wonder of the world

….and my kisses
Grant wishes more delicious than destiny
They want to rest in me
Speaking Fulani to my thighs
Hoping the secrets of civilization
Will somehow fail to sweet temptation
But I stand tall like phallic symbols
They say my smile
Resembles their mommas cooking
Good looking
And tasting like Saturday mornings
Washed down by sips of salvation
I mother nations
Baby boys
Circumsied by circumstance
Step into my circumference
And I will lend you my confort
Bu I export expectations
My nations need to be fathered
Meticulously molded
And scolded
When they step out of line
I don't dare to be different
I'm just different by design
Or divine intervention
My intentions were to remain invisible

But my words got claustrophobic
Bursting out of my throat
Before I choked on reality
It would really be a shame
For someone to
Give me the Heimlich maneuver
Only to find
That it was the truth caught in my throat
So if the good lord be willing
And the creek don't rise
My eyes may wander from the prize
But I stay focused on the race
Through I may stumble
I'll never mumble
Cuz I speak with certain rhythms
Always humble never meek
I may seem usual but
Usually I use that to make change
You can feel it in my nature
It even spells it in my name

I am the womb of man

Buckingham Palace

(A.K.A. "The Regency's")

As I rest on the throne
Of my section 8 palace
I wave to my loyal subjects
In route to the South Side Liquor $ Lotto
No need for a tiara
It might mess up my tracks
And forget a robe
Cuz my royal heinous is up in the finest jeans
Fitting me tighter than me
And my girls use to be
(Before niggas got involved)
Jeans riding the curves
Blessed upon me by motherhood
While concealing the curse
Of stretch marks
That come from being a babies momma
Boosters offer tributes of name brand nonsense
That they barter from the back of a broke down Beretta
Life couldn't be better
I'm a queen
And the projects are my palace

My ladies chase Hennessey
With 40 oz. dreams
Of not having to shake their assess
At a 2 dollar Tuesday
To fill their heads with false self-esteem
And my knights truly believe
That the only reason they hustle
Is to try and fed their seeds
Never realizing
That they've been programmed
To be afraid to succeed

And me
I sit upon my throne
And watch the projects breath
I watch as if they were my sleeping child
So peaceful yet so fickle
Life at its most vulnerable point
Like the soap opera of the slums
Not good enough for some
But this is my palace
And I must bloom
Where I've been planted

1605

(For Carrie O. Bates)

Tonight's sky is a strange shade of blue-black
It sort of reminds me of my Uncle Book Jack,
And the stars sparkle brightly
 Like his dentures that he hardly ever wears
The breeze melts in my mouth
Like Mrs. Annie's sweet potato biscuits
And it touches my face with the softness
Of Miss Titty-Boo's hands
Every step I take reminds me of trips to Bay Smith's house
 To buy 10-cent freeze cups, pickled pig feet
And sunflower seeds.
The scent of Ms. Mary's outhouse still lingers in the August air,
Like late ith Bar-B-Q's on Whitmore rd.

12 Grand babies broke bread

As C.B. fed our spirit

This was her last supper

Time became Judas

Betraying us all

If only I had one last moment

To linger in her laughter.

R.I.P.

(For Neesa)

Like the sweet stench of children in the summer heat
You will forever be embedded in my memory
And just like those scars from that switch
I so carefully chose for my own torture
Those cuts sure hurt when you try to clean them
And even though the streetlights are on
And I can hear my momma yelling my name
I think I'll play for a while
And bathe in the gentle summer breeze of life
Because the winter's not that far away

1st Pregnancy

I have never
Seen your face
Heard your voice
Or felt the warmth of your body
Against my own
But you are my obsession
You are the summit of my existence
I can't remember life
Without your presence
And even though I have never
Held your hand
Inhaled your scent
Or been held hostage by your smile
My love for you
Is still greater than all things

Am I Talking to Myself?

When I speak to God

It speaks back in my own voice

How do you hear it?

Just a Question

If hell does exist

Was it created for us

Or do we make it?

Eucharist

I've been writing
Since I've been writing
Since….
Nouns merged with verbs
Creating complete thoughts
Thinking of ways to engage
What I say with what I mean
Now this may seem simplistic
But I'm being realistic
And reality ain't cool to the socialites
My vocals might
Disturb their distorted thinking
Linking them with the rest of humanity
Living under the canopy
Of other people's perceptions
But Karma, Karma, Karma
Has no exception
What you get is a reflection of who you be
I may not see when you do your dirt
But I cans see when you're buried in it
See I receive knowledge from the earth
And wisdom from the heaven
I hold power like the number 7
So no man will ever divide me from myself
I can only speak what I feel
So I must be touched to know it's real
Because a simulation

Can be as close as masturbation is to sex
Only lacking a key element
I need substance to sustain me
Can you blame me I'm greedy
So if you've got enough to feed the needy
Don't leave me the leftovers
I don't want yesterday's realities
Reheated and served on paper plates
In place of today's truths
My youth is all I have
And father time is trying to molest me
Making me grown before I'm ready
I'd rather rock steady than shake it fast

My hourglass limits my minutes
To grains of sand
I wish I had a beach but life's a bitch
And then you die
Or is life a black girl lost
Carrying the world up on her back
I lack all the right answers
Or even the right questions
So I don't question my blessings
Because tomorrow I could be resting eternally

Burning or lounging in limbo
I often wonder if death is just a symbol
A metaphysical metaphor
Or does it swoop down like the raven
And engulf you forever more
Or are we all destined
To be knocking on heavens door
You can pour me in communion glasses
And pass me around
Because even when by body
Reunites with the ground
My energy
Will still bless this earth residually
There is no end to me

Counting Sacrificial Sheep

I bear these burdens in my belly
Where 5 babies began their journey
Only 3 of them survived
But I guess that's life
Or that's death
Or maybe that's just karma?

I never understood that concept
Until I sacrificed my first seed
They said
I didn't know how to be a momma at 17
And what about all my dreams
Well now I have these nightmares
And I've become accustomed to night air
I'd rather lay awake with my conscious
Than sleep with my demons
So I count sheep and seconds
Until daylight comes to rescue me
But the sun
Just burns my hangover-swollen eyes
And illuminates my pain
So I pray for nightfall
Because the darkness
Is much more forgiving than I could ever be
Somewhere between dusk and dawn
Lies me
With open wounds
A scarred womb
And three heavenly creatures
Who left me with tribal scars
That initiated me into a sisterhood
Ranging from bourgeoisie white women
To girls from the hood
And though we couldn't be more different
We all hold common prayers
Which now consist of the names of
 Baby boys, baby girls, and baby daddies

I can still remember being my daddy's baby
Maybe
If I call him he'll be humming that tune
That tune he sang
The first time he held me
And I can hold that moment in my memory
Just a little bit longer
I can hold that moment
Like my daddy did
The first time

All My Skeletons Won't Fit In My Closet

My innocence is a remembrance
As distant as kemetic queens
I strummed my pain on guitar strings
As he killed me
Just loud enough for no one to hear it
He picked my spirit
Rolling it between his fingers
Flicking it like a booger
My sugar ain't been sweet since
My defense
I was just 10
I cried rivers into the bathtub
As I scrubbed his graffiti
Off my prepubescent vaginal walls
I felt small
Like the semen that ran through my youth
And the truth is
I felt like I was the one in the wrong
Like my song kept skipping
And landing on the same part
My heart was wide open
No words ever spoken
Could verbalize by pain
I would watch the rain
Praying that it could cleanse my soul
But the hole just expanded
As if I was branded for life
My living was in vanity
And my sanity was slowly
Becoming
Submerged
In
Mu
Sorrow

I felt borrowed like had me downs
I wanted grandma's hands
To band-aid my soul
But I never told
Even if he
Sold my babies on southern auction blocks
He could never
Parallel the pain
Of day of the week panties with blood stains
Embedded in my memory
I hated him for so long
By my essence hinders me
From disturbing negative energy
So I just kept remembering
I can't control what men will be like

Seven Years Bad Luck

I used to be pretty
Back before my amber hues became
Dusty browns
Before girls knew running hard would
Make you musty
Back when I had to
Change into my play clothes and
"You can't come over cuz my momma said that I can only have two company's"
Back before I looked into mirrors

I used to see myself in dreams beautiful
Like brown babies
My granny would tell people
That I was going to be an actress
I loved blackberries, wore a Jheri curl
And what the world saw was me
Plain and simple
Without any condiments or side dishes
Wearing my wishes on my sleeve
I spoke what I believed and I was pretty
Back Before I looked into mirrors

When I looked into mirrors
I saw the world reflected on my face
And I couldn't face the music
'Cuz subliminal symphonies
Move me
With the centrifugal force
I've tried bobbing and weaving
But my hips can't move like
The sun, the moon and the planets
And my feet can't stay planted in galaxies
Where my gravity don't pull no one
Before I looked into mirrors
I thought that the universe
Had a uniform understanding
That I am a cosmic queen of kushite decent
But the mirrors just shot back my reflection
Blurred by perceptions
Of what pretty is supposed to be

....nothing like me
See, I was tall
Skinny,
Silly,
Pigeon-toed,
Political princess,
Who played piano and had nice post moves
So they wanted to box me with a title
And call me electric
Because my power is electric
My beauty is deeper than aesthetics,
And sometimes I can be so sweet
I turn healthy men into diabetics
So I break mirrors
And walk barefoot across the glass
Testing the seven year theory
Then let her estrogen energy embrace me
Because lately
It seems as even though
The atmosphere hates me
As I fight against the air I breathe
I pray God please take me
God replies,
"Fear not my child, every day I reshape thee"

When The Rainbow Is Not Enuf
(To Cathy, Billie, Re-Re, Althea, Sabrina, Melia, Sharice, Algie, & Princess Linnie)

Sometimes I fell alone
Like a Jane Doe
Bodies bloodied and bruised
Naked and nameless
Heroines with heroine tracks
Fingers with crack residue
Or booze on her breath

In peace may she rest, because at best

Searching for peace leaves me stressed
So I am sometimes jealous of those women
Who left this world anonymously
Holding their secrets silently
As they suffer no more
She settles the score
Whether housewife or whore
She writes her own history
Envious of their mystery
I see why some colored girls
Considered suicide
Because the rainbow is not enuf
When your blues
Don't blend well with brown skin
And your green don't always
Add up in the end

So men tend to ask me why I don't grin
I wish that I could put them through
Everything I've been
Like how I heard a thousand times
That he'll never do it again
Or how I was molested
At the time I was ten
So I made a promise to myself
That I would never trust men…

…then
I remember Jane Doe and know the power
That my blank expression holds and if I keep
My poker face they can never make me fold
So I reply,
I thought I was smiling

Killing Goliath

I can remember
When I used to spread my soul
From the knew
Maybe it was my need to please
Or my heart screaming
PLEASE NEED ME!
I would let men kneed lumps from my flesh
And in return I would bless them
With the warmth from my breath
So with every exhale cam exile
I would look for easy exits for my emotions
Because I didn't deal well with commotion
Or commitment
I was sure that they would commit me
For committing such sins knowingly
But knowing me
I would sweet talk Satan into sending me
Straight to my savior
And all the angels would be singing
"Don't save her, she don't wanna be saved"
And in a sense they would be right
If I die tonight
I don't want a drip of my destiny
To go untasted
Moments I've wasted
Wishing upon stars
As if the universe owed me a favor
Because sometimes the Universe shows me favor
God treats me as if I'm it's favorite
Maybe I'm from the lineage of David
And that's why I slay giants with mere stones
I stand as a multitude alone

Thank You Marshall Mathers

It's back to reality
Oops there goes gravity
Oops there goes Amber
She won't give up that easy…

See my granny raised me to know that
I am more than birthing babies,
Cooking and cleaning
But men don't always know that
So at times go gotta act crazy
Granny said,
"If he don't fulfill me holistically then fuck him pay me"
I'd rather be one times a bitch
Than three times a lady
No prince charming is gonna slay these
Dragons I'm fighting daily
And no glass slipper will save me
So you can save the fairy tales
And happily ever after
Everything is said and done
The sun will rise in the morning
And if not
I should be the only one mourning

Untitled 1

I've questioned my faith
And I've tested my maker

I've tested my faith
And I've questioned my maker

Still I can't make cents
Out of what makes sense
Cuz' my senses get defenseless
When it comes to dollars and cents
I use to find it odd to praise God
When you can't even pay your rent
And you gave up chocolate for lent
When something good happens
Your're quick to say it's heaven sent
But when the shit this the fans
You don't turn to God you blame man
And you wouldn't hesitate
To bloody your hand
To show loyalty to some land
Sounds like idol worship to me
Bu they say that's what we must do
If we choose to remain free

My county 'tis of thee
Sweet land of liberty
Of thee I sing
Land where my fathers died
Yet I remain a Cimarron
As I simmer on the brink of boiling over
And staining my star spangled banner
Excuse my manners
But I'm just regurgitating
The rhetoric
That I've rehearsed since birth
I was taught to pledge allegiance to a flag

When only I can save me
T.T. is raising our babies
And God forbid you from Haiti
'Cuz they act like them niggas got rabies
I'm not just talking shit
Yo, I live this here daily

And being conscious won't save me
When niggas in my hood think I'm crazy

So I jut
Lay in my bed
And listen to gun spray
Praying one day
One stray
Won't make my babies a statistic
And I'm not being paranoid
Where I'm from it's realistic
And being mystic don't mean shit
To the Gods of ballistics
//you know them trigga happy niggas that be grimmin at me//
//and you they say I act stuck 'cuz I won't give 'em nappy//
//but they wanna chill up in the dugout like they play for the team//
//and when I build 'em a field of dreams//
//then they wanna be traded//

And I hate to sound jaded
 But I'm just happy I made it through all them night I drank too much
Knowing my kidney can't take it
Or all them nights I chilled with niggas
In spots I knew could be raided
But I felt like I was ride or die
So I never debated
Except with God
When I questioned my fate
Or tested it's patience

Girl Fight

This is me
Open
Brown Girl
3 kids
2 babies fathers
College dropout (before Kanye made it sound cool)
Trying to go back
Trying to get back
Trying to step back
And take on life from a different angle
Maybe this time
I can grab it by the horns and hold on tight
Maybe this time I'll Vaseline my face and put up a fight
This time I won't apologize or compromise
I'll compose symphonies that I can dance to
And won't give a damn
If anyone else can catch the beat
From academia to street
I'm the poster child for girls gone wild
But I'm not flashing tits
I'm throwing fits
Teaching my sisters to fish
And I wish somebody would step in my path
I would unleash the wrath
Of us war torn women
Tired of fighting for Eve's innocence
Tired of fighting for Cleopatra's clitoris
Tired of fighting to be feminine and feminist
Tired of fighting

Diary II

The Revolution Will Not Be Available On Bootleg

Big Black Truths

I am the sum of all fears
The boogie mans baby
Black
Belly full of riotous words
Proud and unapologetic
Not claiming to be prophetic
I'm just calling it like I see
Speaking these words
So that they will reach into someone's mind
Becoming nightmares
Haunting their every thought with the truth
Creating insomniacs who refuse to sleep
Are dreams
And we need Action
Words are just rhythms
Tickling eardrums
Unless they move bodies
And tantalize minds
Resulting in a revolutionary waltz
Attention: Life has no dress rehearsal
Although practice makes perfect
We must reflect on our purpose
Because you eyes aren't promised
Sunday's sunrise to save your soul
Time waits for no man
So like a nomad I am never stagnant
Magnetic forces try to pull me back
Hoping that I believe myths
On how I am inclined to fail
Based on genetics
So white destiny is undressing me
I look for an escape route
But my legs are too short to run from God

And even if I could
Who would I run to
I would be running
Just for the sake of running
And in spite of reality
Hyperventilating hypocrisy
Because faith ain't based on democracy
So I do what I sent for
You can call me destiny's house nigga

For the lack of a better figure of speech
So as I speak in the tongue of understanding
The only thing to fear is me
Because I am the boogie mans baby
Black
Bottled up with pride
Shaken up with ignorance
And ready to explode at any moment
Spraying knowledge
And staining you little white lies
With my big black truth

For Uncle Ric, Roy II and W.B.T.

I was too much for them to handle
I was
Too young
Too ghetto
Too proud
I looked to many white men in the eye
And told them what I thought about them
I bumped my music too loud
And it was too powerful
So now they write tickets for that too
They say I be disturbing the peace
I just feel like I be deserving some peace
And them lyrics over beats
Just show how some niggas can get a piece
Of that American pie
That they keep waving in my face
Then when we can't afford bread
They say let them niggas eat cake
So I star half-baked and flip wright to try and create opportunity
But between you and me
Tis shit feel like a conspiracy
Like I was set up from the second
Sperm reached my mommas cervix
It's like they invented hard time
Just so niggas could serve it
And they brought crack to the inner city
Just so niggas could serve it
The when you get caught and locked up
They say that nigga deserved it
They would rather see me depressed than acknowledge my success
Bu no matter how much they curse me
It won't work 'cuz I'm blessed

Once I realize my power It only increases their fear of me
'Cuz their sons try and mirror me
Their daughters want to get near to me
So in attempts to break my spirit
They take away everything that's dear to me
But even locked away in silence
God keeps on hearing me
When I think I've hit rock bottom
God keeps on hearing me
When all I have left is a whisper
God keeps on hearing me
God keeps on hearing
God keeps on
God keeps
God
Keeps
On…

I Prefer Kool-Aide

I don't even like coffee
So why should I be limited
To performing in coffee shops
In front of New Age
So called conscious cats
Rocking dreads and backpacks
And drinking coffee
As if those were the status symbols of depth

I prefer performing in front of
Middle Eastern owned liquor stores
In black "hoods
Stores that have a kitchen in the back
And serve soul food without the soul

I prefer performing
For dudes with hood names
Like Bay Boy or Turk
Men who's real name you never knew
Or even bothered to ask
Until you read his obituary and thought
Damn,
I've known this man for ten years
And never bothered to ask his real name
I wonder if any of our conversations
Meant shit or were they just a waste of spit
Maybe I wasted some of his
10,911,600 minutes that he had on the planet
I don't know you do the math

I prefer performing for old heads
Who lived revolution
Old heads who know the solution
But their words fall upon deaf ears
People who patiently sacrificed
And strategically made moves
Because somewhere
Embedded in their subconscious
Was the first rule of physics
Every action must have a reaction

So as I try to keep my generation afloat
We all go to heaven on a little rowboat
I hope I don't get seasick
I've got to pee
Quit tickling me with deep beats
And shallow rhymes
You act like you're afraid
To simulate peoples minds
Afraid that you might find something

I don't even like coffee
It give me migraines
Mental jungles thicker than
A 13-year old black girls natural hair
Which she relaxes and presses
Because society associates that thick hair
With a thick mind
But all she sees on videos is thin hair
And thick behinds
And that was just fine with her momma
Who hated combing that kitchen
So she permed her hair when she was 5
Her mother hated that kitchen
She sat in listening to people say
How pretty her sister was
Because she had "Good Hair"
It was the same kitchen
Where on any given Friday
Her mother would sit
And talk about how men ain't shit
It was the same kitchen
Where every morning lingered the
Thick
Black
Aroma
Of Coffee

I Can't Carry A Tune

Did I ever tell you I use to wish I could sing
I was about 8 or 9 or 16, or maybe even 21
I use to wish that
The melodies that made men melt
Were impregnated into my vocal cords
And born to my thick tawny lips
I wished that I could
Harmonize with the heavens
And sing acapella with the angels
Orcastrating opal operas
Creating oral-gasms
I longed to hear, ""that girl sure can sing"
Any time that I blessed the trees
With the carbon monoxide that I exhale
When I sing

Did I ever tell you I use to wish I could sing

I wanted
African chants
Negro Spirituals
Gospel tunes
Blues hits
R & B hymns
And hip-hop choruses
To boil in my belly
Erupting through my trachea
Slowly simmering out of my mouth
Did I ever tell you I use to wish I could sing

I wished that I could sing
With the voice of the slaves
Miscarried from the womb of civilization

I wished that I could sing
With the voice of mothers born to breed
Whose babies were stolen and sold
And they had to cope
Because black women
Weren't allowed to go crazy

I wished that I could sing
With the voice of the black farmhands
Migrating from one slave system to another
Bamboozled into believing that
Building Buicks
Was better than building black brains

I wished that I could sing
With a voice so loud
That it went back in time
To comfort Assata's imprisoned body
9 months ripe with the will of God

I wished that I could sing
For all of my undereducated
College conditioned people
Who believe the struggle is over
So they give up the fight
But thieves don't always rob in the night
They sometimes blind with the light
I use to wish I could sing
But no I just write.

Words Of My Father

The straight-ahead keeps spinning around
Making my vision blur again
I'm sure you've once been in
The state of mind I'm in

I see step less glass towers
Leading to the infinity
Of my hopes and dreams
While passing elevator shafts to security
The nine-to-five boredom
All of the normal things

I never want to shoot a gun
Or pull an arrow string
Needle my veins or blow my mind
No, none of the normal things

I want all to see truth in plain clear words
Without loop holes, deceptions, or schemes
I want mankind to be just one kind
And not one of the normal things
The straight-ahead keeps spinning around
Making my vision blur again
I'm sure you've once been in
The state of mind I'm in
And if you have and didn't change
You should cry and never sing
But do as you want and so will I
That's one of the normal things

On The Back Of Milk Cartons

Poetry is my native tongue
I breathe hard with one lung
I donated my other one to the struggle
I huddle up with hood rats
And hold round table discussions
But the percussion
Keeps raping their eardrums
As beats box with verbs
The streets stand in silence
My words slice the wind
With the violence of violin concertos
I try to keep my concentration
But the good vibrations have me
Day dreaming and thinking of
U
N
I
T
Y can't they get it
Seems like I'm
Speaking into the windy city's streets
At 4am during February's Fury
Forgetting that the truth
Sometimes gets lost in translation
So I must transform my words
And become an optimist in my prime
Fighting time trying to make overtures
In my ovaries
Street symphonies
Become soundtracks
To breakfast at Tiffany's
And between sound bites
I try and spoon-feed her dreams
About things other than him

Because if you look at the whole scheme
He's as minute as a minuet
A one night standing ovation
Is nothing in comparison
To a lifelong appreciation
Of the music made by your spirit
Bu the bass line keep her in bondage
So I just blow away my gripes
Through my peace pipe
As I mediate on how
To help my sisters levitate
From the abyss of theses city streets
But before they can feel what I speak
My works got abducted by the beat

Diary III

Cupid Must Be Cross-Eyed

Something Like A Love Poem

I've been simply blessed by your simplicity
By not having to analyze our connection
We're deeper than that
You're like my brother another mother
Maybe we were in love in another lifetime
Maybe you were my mother
And I was your seed
And we were connected by our lifeline
Your scent is sweeter
Than the smell of mornings
When I wake cloaks in your spirit
Inhaling you calm
Is like my hearts aromatherapy
And your voice is chicken soup for my soul
You are perfections reelection
Dipped in hot cocoa
Milk chocolate never semi-sweet
And your feet
Have traveled eternally through my thoughts
Every doubt I ever had about myself
You bring me peace
A midsummer night's breeze
Softly caressing my love
You are my man on the moon
Watching over me
As a Shepard watches over his sheep
And as you sleep
I watch you with the satisfaction of knowing
That every ounce of my being
Belongs with you
When I listen to your heartbeat
It sounds like
The instrumental version
Of the world spinning on its axis
Like our souls embracing the sunshine
And the moon reflecting

Thanks For Laughing At My Joke

I was born alone
And I will die alone
So if I spend every moment
In between then in solitude
I will only be continuing my cycle
No I don't need closure
We can leave this wide open
You owe me nothing
I will take lesion learned as ransom
Nothing in life is random
With memories in hand
I will humbly bow out
White flag waving
No use behaving like children
We must think about our children
We must think about our children
Through all of this
Tearing down and rebuilding
I've changes so much
Tat I may never again be right for you
But I will continue to write for you
I love you in spite of you

Seeing you smile
Makes me thankful for the gift of sight
While knowing I may never complete you
Keeps me up nights
My tears are not only out of sadness
But also fear
I am afraid that down the road
Destiny had divided our paths
Making you and I the past
So if this wasn't meant to last
The fact that I was able
To experience your laugh
Is one of the greatest gifts I have

We'll Be Butterfly's

It was the middle of July
But the heat that I was feeling wasn't
Coming from the sun
It was coming from your tongue
This was feeling like the matrix
If it was you were the one
I was convinced our conversation
Wouldn't lead to much
But when I saw you lick your lips
I could feel myself blush
I know I shouldn't trust
A man I barely even know
With secrets I normally keep hush
Then you licked your lips again
And I thought damn this is a must
You made me feel comfortable
Which isn't usual to me
But I was just using you for me
I needed to feel wanted
And your touch tickled my ego
While your voice sang sweet temptations
Past my better judgment
I hoped you wouldn't judge me
I just want you to love me
But only for one night
 I knew it wasn't right
And in spite I bit into forbidden fruit
Letting the juice drip from my lips
Because just to feel you kiss felt like kismet
Like we were celestially connected
A constellation
Isis and Osiris
Sipping Milky Way libations
Loving without earthly boundaries
You have eternally bound me
Within you I have found me

Word's Can't Explain

You Make Me feel so inadequate so average
I feel humbled in your presence like you were Jesus of Nazareth
I'm baffled
I never knew that love could be so effortless
Yet have so much prevalence
I hold you in the highest reverence
You're heaven sent
In spirit you exemplify divinity
My own Holy Trinity
I know understand serendipity
This was meant to be…
I try ad balance what I want for you and what you need
In me God planted you precious seeds
But the fruit you bear isn't up to me
I feel helpless
And I wish I could help more
But I know that holding
Your hand for too long
Won't have you strong enough to stand on you own two
I realize that I don't own you
So in the end I hope you're better because of what I've shown you
And I hope what I've shown you was worth seeing

Beyond Fear

I'm not even afraid anymore
I have gotten out of the habit of using common sense as my excuse not to become involved emotionally
Right now I feel like totally taking off my chainmail and submitting to amour
I just want to explore the option without stopping myself halfway
God led me down this pathway
So I'm praying for safe passage and a pleasant journey
But I think that I have fallen
Despite the caution signs I keep walking and wanting more by the moment
How it happened is a mystery
I'm not sure how we got here but this is where I want to be
And I'm not even afraid anymore...
I don't even care if you share these sentiments
Because love is in bloom so this must be Nirvana
And right now I'm just enjoying everything about you
I may not speak the words but I am in too deep to be without you
So no matter how I tip toe around it
The safety net is gone and what is left is me and you
And I'm not even afraid anymore...
Not scared of what may or may not transpire
I'm tired of being in love with you subliminally
You entice me mentally
Please me physically
Mesh with me spiritually
All of the fear in me has been removed
And replaced with hope and wholehearted attempts at forever
...whatever that is...
I just want to live in your presence
Learning from our imperfections and growing by the second
My only weapons being patience, love, trust, understanding, and forgiveness
I want to witness love in its entirety
So I'm closing my eyes, opening my heart, and letting go
And I'm not even afraid anymore...
Even if this all ends in disaster I'm satisfied with how right it feels right now
I'm willing to sacrifice my comfort for a genuine experience of being in love Above any boundaries or expectations and outside of the realm of reason
And beyond the existence of fear...

Sun Salutation

Engaged in the sweet nectar of the morning
4am doesn't seem so early when you're kneeling
The moonlight more luminous when you're healing
A flickering lantern on my way
As I'm feeling through the darkness...and it doesn't scare me
I sip coffee and wait for dawn
Drawn to meditation
By air perfumed with sandalwood and Egyptian musk
I don't rush it
I'm lingering in the dark of morning
Full from far
No one could steal this still
Relaxed by the slight chill at daybreak and I don't want to sleep
I want to let the sunlight creep past curtains
And court me with it's warmth
I'm smiling
And the only reason for my joy is that
I have been blessed enough to experience another moment
Another mystical montage narrated by the creator
I am grateful for this present
It's what I've always wanted...

The poetry of being
A sundrenched sonnet tattooed on my spirit
I recite it aloud so that everyone can hear it
Baffled by its simplicity is why some people fear it
Each word a lyric lamenting my existence
Resistance only makes the journey harder
The potter won't stop molding,
Worn down from holding on I surrender to it's will
This is all just a wheel
A constantly morphing metaphor forevermore
I salute the sun in gratitude to the Almighty
It's slivers of radiance remind me that
I am everything and nothing simultaneously
So humbly I greet the day open and receptive
Prepared for its peaks and valleys
Which neither define or validate
They just offer me new spaces to grow and explore freely
Because no matter how steep the mountain or how low the grove
I know that there is always another chance for redemption with every new sunrise...

Fallen

You are a dream
Wrapped in a fairy tail
Covered in comfort and smothered in serenity
I can't explain our chemistry
You are a mystery
A whimsical whirlwind of wonderful
I'm most comfortable in your presence, it's like heaven
Our connection is near perfection
If you use love as a weapon I will meet death any second
I've fallen

IV

Life

Amongst The Living

I visit the cemetery when I have urges to do things that are self-destructive or counterproductive…I don't know any one buried there but it helps me to clear my head and think straight…it helps me to remember that some choices are so final and that something's we do have everlasting consequences. I also remember that I still have a chance to change and to be better and the people buried there no longer have that luxury…it also shocks me the monuments we dedicate to people when they are gone while we don't give them the time and attention that they deserve when they are alive…if I haven't told u lately self…I love u…and to those reading this I love u too…live in peace!

Amber Hasan
Visit My Web Site At:
www.amberswriting.com

Follow Me On Twitter @**AmbersWriting**
Follow Me On Instagram @ **Amber_Hasan**
Follow Me On Pinterest @**AmberHasanPins**
Check Out My Blog @**www.amberhasan.blogspot.com**

www.ingramcontent.com/pod-product-compliance
Lightning Source LLC
Chambersburg PA
CBHW071740040426
42446CB00012B/2404